SOLD!
The Origins of Money and Trade

SOLD!

The Origins of Money and Trade

RP Prepared by Geography Department

Runestone Press ◆ Minneapolis

RUNESTONE PRESS • RUNESTONE

rune (ro͞on) *n* **1 a :** one of the earliest written alphabets used in northern Europe, dating back to A.D. 200; **b :** an alphabet character believed to have magic powers; **c :** a charm; **d :** an Old Norse or Finnish poem. **2 :** a poem or incantation of mysterious significance, often carved in stone.

Sold! The Origins of Money and Trade is a fully revised and updated edition of *Coins of the Ancient World,* a title previously published by Lerner Publications Company. The text is completely reset in 12/15 Albertus, and new photographs and captions have been added.

Thanks to Dr. Guy Gibbon, Department of Anthropology, University of Minnesota, for his help in preparing this book.

Words in **bold** type are listed in a glossary that starts on page 61.

Library of Congress Cataloging–in–Publication Data
  Sold!: the origins of money and trade / prepared by Geography Department, Runestone Press.
    p. cm—(Buried Worlds)
  Includes index.
  ISBN 0–8225–3206–9 (lib. bdg.)
  1. Coins, Ancient—History—Juvenile literature. 2. Commerce—History—To 500—Juvenile literature. [1. Money—History. 2. Commerce—History.] I. Runestone Press. Geography Dept. II. Series.
CJ233.S65 1994
737.4'09—dc20   93–37782
                                                      CIP
                                                      AC

Manufactured in the United States of America
1 2 3 4 5 6 – I/JR – 99 98 97 96 95 94

CONTENTS

HOW MONEY BEGAN

Every day we use coins, paper money, checks, credit cards, and computer transactions to buy goods and services. We purchase items such as clothes, food, books, and movie tickets. Almost all our daily needs are obtained with money.

Thousands of years ago, people did not have money. Individual families and entire villages worked together to meet all their needs. They grew their own crops and hunted animals for their meat and hides. Ancient people built their own houses and even cured their own illnesses as best they could. If a family needed something that it could not produce—such as a special medicine—members would pay the provider with things, such as blankets, jewelry, grain, or livestock. This exchange of goods and services for other goods and services is called **barter.**

Ten thousand years ago, most people were hunters and gatherers who lived in small settlements and met all their needs by bartering. Over time, people cut down trees to build houses and cleared forests to create farmland. In the process, the small settlements grew into large villages.

As populations increased, villages became towns and towns became cities. Many urban people stopped farming and began to specialize in one kind of activity, such as healing the sick, building houses,

Archaeologists (scientists who dig up and study ancient objects) discovered this hoard (hidden supply) of silver in the Middle Eastern country of Israel. The ancient Israelites traded precious metals, such as gold and silver, for goods and services.

or making jewelry. Soon ancient city dwellers relied on one another for food, housing, and clothing.

As cities expanded, bartering became more difficult. If a family needed a new table, for example, members might ask a carpenter to build one and offer grain in exchange. But what if the carpenter already had enough grain and really wanted a bead necklace? If the family did not have a bead necklace to offer, members would have to barter with someone else for the beads to pay the carpenter. In this way, bartering became complicated.

On the Pacific Islands, some traditional cultures use feather money as part of important ceremonies, such as weddings. Islanders make their money by decorating long coils of plant fiber with small feathers. Ancient cultures exchanged many other natural items, including pebbles and shells.

Issued in about 45 B.C., this Roman coin shows the head of the goddess Juno Moneta, whose name gives us the English word money.

WHAT'S IN A NAME?

The ancient Romans believed that gods and goddesses controlled all aspects of everyday life. The most powerful Roman goddess was Juno, the queen of the gods. Juno held many titles. Roman women often worshiped her as Juno Lucina, the goddess of childbirth. She also served as Juno Fortuna, the goddess of fate.

In 390 B.C., according to legend, Juno's sacred geese alerted the Romans that the Gauls (a Celtic group from what is now France) had attacked and were setting fire to Rome. This protective act earned Juno the title Moneta, meaning warning. To honor the goddess, the Romans dedicated a temple to her as Juno Moneta. Early Roman coin makers set up a workshop near her temple. Later, places where Roman coins were made came to be called *moneta,* a name that also gives us the English word *money.*

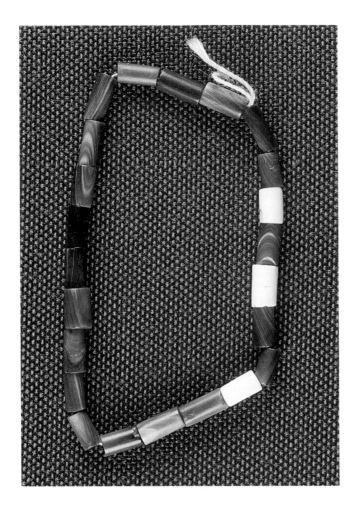

An early artisan crafted these beads from stone, which ancient people used for money.

From Ingots to Coins

To simplify their method of exchange, ancient people invented money by placing fixed values on certain items, such as pebbles, shells, beads, and even feathers. The most common forms of money in ancient times, however, were gold and silver. These metals were hard to find and difficult to mine. As a result, their value was high. Sellers eagerly accepted gold or silver in exchange for their goods or services.

At first, ancient people used lumps of precious metal—called **ingots**—as money. Buyers carried ingots of gold, silver, and bronze (a mixture of copper and tin). Since ingots were formed in various shapes and sizes, their worth depended on their weight.

The first records of people using ingots as money come from Mesopotamia, a region of the Middle East that covers what are now eastern Syria, southeastern Turkey, and most of Iraq. The Sumerians, who inhabited Mesopotamia from about

4000 B.C. to 2300 B.C., kept track of payments in silver for land rent and for local taxes.

Ingots posed some problems for ancient merchants. Even if the piece was weighed, sellers could not know the true value from appearance alone. For example, ingots made of gold—the most valuable metal—were usually mixed with silver because pure gold is too brittle to keep its shape. But merchants had difficulty judging exactly what percentage of silver a gold ingot contained.

The problem of determining the content or purity of ingots was partly solved by stamping them with **seals.** Each seal displayed a description of the metal content, as well as a declaration of its weight. If ancient traders recognized the seal and believed that the information was correct, they did not need

Buyers once carried lumps of precious metals called ingots. The value of these bronze ingots, which archaeologists found in Israel, depended on their weight.

to weigh or examine the ingot. For this reason, stamped ingots were convenient and helped buyers to make quick purchases.

Nevertheless, many merchants continued to weigh ingots. Because most seals covered only a small part of the ingot, people often shaved off some of the metal to make into another ingot. When these shavings were removed, the ingot lost some of its worth, and the merchant did not receive the expected amount of money. Despite these problems, stamped ingots were an important step in the development of coins.

The Invention of Coins

In the ancient Middle East and in the region surrounding the Mediterranean Sea—including southern Europe and northern Africa—the use of money flourished along busy trading routes. As a result, ancient

Ancient ingots came in many different shapes and sizes. This hoard contained small loops and large lumps of silver.

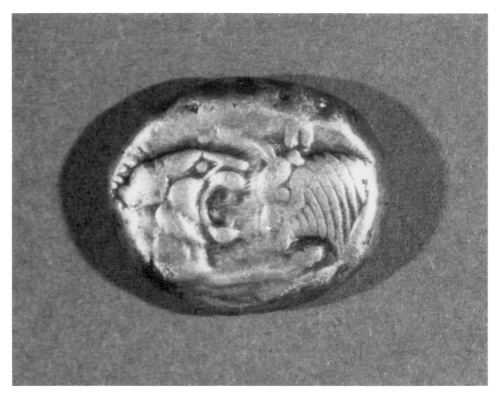

In about 700 B.C., the Lydians began minting coins called staters. Stater is the name used for coins that come from ancient Greek city-states. This silver stater, which was crafted about 560 B.C., depicts a lion confronting a bull.

coins have turned up among the ruins of many ancient cities. **Archaeologists** (scientists who dig up and study ancient objects) have also discovered coins in tombs and at the bottom of the sea.

Archaeologists believe that the world's first coins were made or **minted** around 700 B.C. in Lydia, a kingdom in Asia Minor (modern Turkey). The first coins were very similar to ingots. Formed into round lumps, they were stamped with crude seals that declared weight and purity. But well-minted coins carried two large seals that covered most of the surface. This made it more difficult for someone to shave off the metal without also cutting off part of the seal.

For a while, the Lydians and their nearest neighbors were the only ancient people making coins and using them for trade. But the Lydians began to grow wealthy, and their influence quickly spread. Lydian traders brought coins to Greece in the west, to the Middle East in the south, and to Persia (modern Iran) in the east. During the fifth century B.C., coins gradually replaced ingots and became widespread throughout much of the Mediterranean region and the Middle East.

WEIGHTS, MEASURES, AND VALUES

When coins first came into use, minters made them by hand, one by one. As a result, it was unusual to find two coins of the exact same weight and appearance. Early coins were made of precious metals, so even a small variation in weight could make a significant difference in the value of each coin. For this reason, many people did not trust seals and instead continued to measure the worth of their coins by weight. Another reason that merchants did not put away their scales is that ingots were still in use.

Because merchants continued to weigh money, ancient minters saw no need to be precise in their work. Although some mints (factories where coins are made) tried to standardize the weights of their coins, others continued to produce coins of various weights.

For example, ancient coins minted in Athens varied less than 10 percent in weight. Coins with similar seals that were minted in other cities showed a 40-percent weight difference. In modern times, that would be the same as having a $20 bill that might be worth anywhere from $10 to $30, depending on the bill's thickness.

In ancient times, honest merchants used a set method to weigh ingots or coins to determine their value. The sellers attached metal pans of equal weight *(fourth row)* to scales. Then they placed the ingots or coins in one scale pan and added stones *(rows one, two, three, and five),* **which had known weights,** to the other pan until the two sides balanced. Because each type of metal had a set value by weight, merchants could settle on how much the coins or ingots were worth.

Gold, Silver, and Electrum

The Lydians minted the first coins from **electrum,** a mixture of gold and silver. Pale yellow in color, electrum is a natural metal found in the ground. In later times, ancient minters made coins from many different metals, including pure gold, pure silver, and bronze. In general, gold was worth more than silver, and silver was worth more than bronze. But the value stamped on a coin was based mainly on the coin's size. For instance, a very large silver coin was worth more than a tiny gold coin.

Although electrum was a beautiful combination of gold and silver, it held certain disadvantages. All electrum did not contain the same proportions of gold and silver. Since gold was more valuable, electrum coins containing more silver were worth less.

The proportion of metals affected the coin's color, which the ancient Lydians used to determine its value. The average electrum coin was worth about 75 percent of a

Traveling merchants could fold this early wooden scale for easy transport.

By about 550 B.C.,
people in the
Mediterranean
region had learned
to separate the gold
from the silver
naturally found in
electrum, an alloy
(mixture) of the two
metals. As a result,
minters could use
pure gold *(right)* **and**
pure silver *(above)* **in
their coins.**

This Egyptian wall painting dates from the fourteenth-century B.C. and depicts a merchant weighing gold rings, which were used as money. The rarity and durability of gold has made this metal the most valuable since ancient times.

This ancient stone weight, equals the weight of four shekels. The shekel is still used as a unit of money in modern Israel.

pure gold coin of equal weight. But dark yellow electrum, which contained a higher proportion of gold, was worth more than 75 percent, and pale electrum was worth less.

The values of gold and silver in relation to one another had a standard worth. An ounce (28 grams) of gold equaled just over 13 ounces (369 grams) of silver. This ratio remained steady for many years and was known throughout the ancient world.

Major events—such as wars, conquests, and the discovery of new trade routes—sometimes increased or decreased the availability of precious metals and changed the ratio. One such change occurred just before 300 B.C., when Alexander the Great, the king of Macedonia (an area in present-day Greece) overran the Persian Empire, which controlled much of western Asia. Alexander then created a kingdom that stretched from the Mediterranean Sea to India.

The Persian rulers had mined gold on a large scale and had accumulated vast treasures in their palaces. Alexander and his companions, who captured these palaces as well as the gold mines, brought much of this wealth back

A portrait of the Greek king Alexander the Great appears on this coin from 323 B.C. Alexander conquered the lands between the Mediterranean Sea and India, spreading Greek coinage to the region.

to Greece. As gold became abundant, it was not considered so precious and its value dropped. After Alexander's conquest, 1 ounce (28 grams) of gold came to be worth 10 ounces (284 grams) of silver.

In modern times, most coins are not made from valuable metals like gold and silver. Coins from the United States, for example, contain different combinations of copper, zinc, and nickel. Modern governments issue these types of coins

Alexander the Great (far left) and Darius (far right), the ruler of Persia (modern Iran), met in a fierce battle in 333 B.C. After his victory, Alexander seized Persia's gold mines and palace treasures. Because gold quickly became more common, its value began to fall.

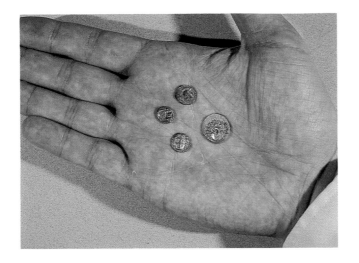

Ancient minters produced very small silver coins (left) to use as change for more valuable coins. But these small pieces were difficult to handle, and minters eventually crafted larger coins from bronze (below), a less expensive metal.

with seals that specify a value. Although the metals in modern coins are not very valuable, the money is always worth the amount that the government stamps on the coin.

Small Change

Because the first ancient coins were made mainly of precious metals, it was difficult to mint them in low

The Japanese government guarantees that this coin is worth its stamped amount—50 yen (the Japanese unit of money). Because governments back the value of their money, most modern coins contain mixtures of metals that are less valuable than gold or silver.

values, such as the pennies, nickels, and dimes of modern times. Even fairly small-sized coins made of precious metals were too valuable to use for purchasing inexpensive items.

Ancient minters eventually began to make tiny silver coins in many different sizes and weights to be used as small change. The largest of these coins could fit on a pencil eraser, and the smallest could pass through the eyelet of a laced shoe. Their small size made these coins awkward to handle and easy to lose. In time, minters began to use less valuable metals, such as copper or bronze, to make low-value coins.

DATING WITH COINS

When archaeologists excavate a site, they identify layers of earth called strata. Each layer, or stratum, represents a different period of time, with the earliest layers at the bottom and the latest layers at the top. For example, one layer might be thick, containing the foundations of buildings and the belongings of people who once lived on the site. The next stratum, however, might be simply a thin layer of dirt blown over the site by the wind. Part of an archaeologist's job is to figure out when each stratum was formed.

Finding a coin within a stratum can help an excavator date a site because minters stamped many ancient coins with the names or images of rulers. From historical documents, archaeologists know when these leaders were in power.

Other coins contain recognizable words or symbols, and some even bear actual dates. As a result, historians, coin collectors, and archaeologists have been able to identify when and where most ancient coins were minted. Excavators can use this information for easy reference when dating a stratum.

Although each coin can be traced to a specific time period, this date cannot always be assigned to the stratum in which the coin was found. Ancient coins often circulated for many years. For this reason, the layer containing a coin cannot be earlier than the date of the coin, but the stratum could be later. In this way, coins help archaeologists narrow the time frame for when ancient people inhabited different sites.

Excavators unearth ancient coins at a site in Israel.

EARLY MINTING METHODS

In modern times, coins are made with the help of machines. Mints can produce large numbers of coins with speed and efficiency. Only four mints, for example, supply all the coins used in the entire United States. In ancient times, when coins were crafted by hand, more mints were needed to supply the population with money. Despite modern technological advances, however, the basic method of minting coins has changed little since ancient times.

Minting Ancient Coins

Although many coins were made of pure gold or pure silver, ancient minters often added stronger metals to make coins more durable. For instance, minters added small quantities of silver and copper to gold. Bronze was mixed with silver, and lead and zinc were blended with bronze. These metals had to be melted down and mixed together before any other work could be done.

Ancient minters poured the melted metal mixtures into molds, or **casts.** Most ancient casts consisted of two parts that fit together and resembled an egg carton with a flat top. The bottom section had rows of disk-shaped spaces. Connecting the spaces were narrow channels that allowed melted metal to flow evenly throughout the cast.

Ancient minters used a two-piece tool called a die (above) *to stamp designs on coins. Dies with deep, detailed carvings produced the finest imprints.*

The top half of the cast held a funnel that attached to the channel and was open to the outside.

After clamping the two halves of the cast together, minters or their assistants poured the hot metal mixture through the funnel until all the spaces were full. After the cast cooled, the coin maker opened it and removed the metal disks. At this point, the smooth, blank disks—called **flans**—were still connected by the narrow strip of metal that had formed in the channel. Rather than separating the flans at this stage, ancient minters left them connected in neat rows so that they could be easily handled during the next phase of minting.

Striking is the process of stamping a design onto the flat sides of a flan. Ancient minters struck each side of a flan with a metal stamp, or **die,** that was much harder than

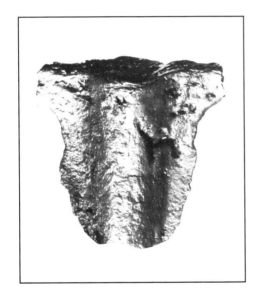

Early coin makers poured liquid metal into casts (below) through small funnels (left). This bronze funnel could withstand the high temperatures of melted gold or silver.

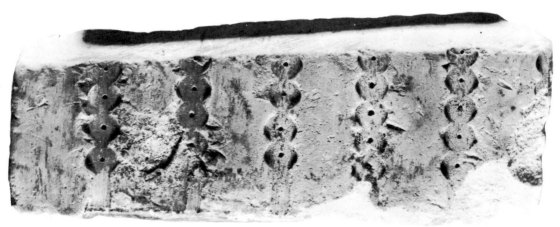

Early minters used tongs (left) to handle heated metal and heavy hammers (right) to strike dies.

the metal of the flan itself. For soft gold coins, dies were usually made of bronze, a metal of medium hardness. But for sturdier silver and bronze coins, the dies had to be crafted of very hard metals, such as iron or even steel. These harder metals created clear impressions on the flans. If the metal of a die was not hard enough, the die could be ruined during the striking process.

Before striking the flans, the minter softened them slightly in a hot furnace. The softened metal

SHELLING IT OUT

At least 3,000 years ago, people in Africa, Asia, and Australia were using shiny shells called cowries as a means of exchange. These shells are found in the shallow, tropical waters of the Indian Ocean, which borders the three continents. Although cowries come in many different shapes and sizes, ancient people chose small shells for trade. The use of these glossy cowries as money was so common that scientists named them *Cuprea moneta,* or money cowries.

Archaeologists believe that ancient people liked the beauty of the shells. Moreover, cowries had a uniform shape, size, and value, so people readily accepted them in trade. Since each cowrie was worth the same amount, people simply counted out the shells to make a purchase. Ancient people often drilled holes in the shells and strung them to carry easily.

Ancient people in Africa, Asia, and Australia used small cowrie shells as money.

28

Workers at this sixteenth-century mint still employed many ancient techniques. Coins were cast to speciflc sizes and struck with hammers and dies. The minter (behind the back counter) **weighed the coins to assure their value.**

allowed the die to make a deep, clear impression. While the flans heated, the minter prepared the dies. One die was set into an **anvil,** a solid platform on which metal could be pounded into shape. Most ancient anvils were tree stumps. The minter held the second die in one hand and a heavy hammer in the other hand.

When the flans reached the correct temperature, the minter's assistant broke them apart. One by one, the assistant set the flans on top of the die in the anvil. The minter placed the other die on top of the hot flan so that the flan was sandwiched between the two dies. The minter then hit the die with a swift, sure stroke of the hammer.

The Roman emperor Vespasian appears on this well-struck coin.

Without a moment's hesitation, the minter lifted the die, the assistant moved the next flan into position, the die came down again, and another blow would fall.

One after another, the rapidly cooling flans were placed between the two dies and struck with the minter's hammer. With each blow, both sides of a coin were stamped with the intended seal. This process continued until all the flans were made into newly minted coins.

Art and Style

The monetary value of coins depended on such things as the composition of the metal and the weight of the coin. The artistic quality depended on other factors. Well-struck coins had deep, clear impressions. In some cases, skilled artists designed the dies.

During ancient times, the same coin was often produced by numerous small mints. Large empires controlled mints in many cities, towns, and villages. At different points in history, for example, the Greeks and the Romans ruled much of the area along the Mediterranean Sea. The smaller Greek and Roman settlements produced copies of coins minted in the large capital cities.

Although coins minted in smaller cities were supposed to be exact duplicates of those minted in the capitals, they were often vastly inferior in quality. There is a great difference, for instance, in the image

A coin's quality can help archaeologists identify its origin. Coins from the eastern Mediterranean port of Sidon (above left) and the imperial capital of Rome (below left) are clear and detailed. Coins from smaller mints, such as the ancient cities of Accho (above right) and Ashqelon (below right), are of lesser quality.

of Alexander the Great that appears on tetradrachm coins minted in large Greek cities and the same head as it appears on the tetradrachms of Accho, an ancient port located in present-day Israel. Tetradrachms equaled four drachmas, the monetary unit of Greece.

During the rule of the Romans, poor crafting in small, local mints was a common problem. Coins minted in Rome display a portrait of the Roman emperor Hadrian with well-defined features. But the same portrait appearing on a coin minted in the ancient seaport of Ashqelon (located on the southwestern coast of modern Israel) is of poor quality. Hadrian's face is crudely designed and almost

unrecognizable, perhaps because the mint at Ashqelon did not care about accurately portraying a distant ruler.

During ancient times, each mint tended to have its own style and its own standards of quality. The differences between mints were often so clear that modern experts can examine an ancient coin and tell not only how old it is and where it came from but even in which mint it was struck.

Forgeries

Coins were invented so that the seal, which specified the purity and weight of each coin's metal, could be trusted. The work of ancient mints was an important step in the development of a reliable money system. Yet almost as soon as coins became widespread, people began to make fakes. Forgers knew that a coin with a familiar seal would be accepted without being carefully weighed or examined.

When archaeologists or other experts closely examine ancient coins, they often find that edges were cut, leaving small, wedge-shaped marks. Because fake coins, or forgeries, were common, ancient people carved into the edges to check the coin's authenticity. Forgers tried to pass off fakes made of cheap metals covered with gold or silver.

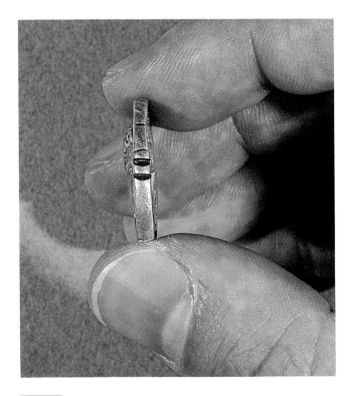

An ancient merchant probably cut into the edge of this coin to make sure it contained pure silver.

Residents of the Pacific island of Yap display their traditional stone money. The ancient Yap made stones as large as 12 feet (4 meters) wide.

THE ISLAND OF STONE MONEY

The enormous stone money made by the early inhabitants of Yap earned this Pacific island the nickname the "Island of Stone Money." Located in the western Pacific Ocean, Yap is the largest of the 14 Yap Islands. About 5,000 people are scattered across the fertile land of this island group.

The ancient Yap made their money from aragonite, a type of limestone found on the islands. Shaped into flat disks with holes in the centers, the stone money ranged in size from 20 inches (50 centimeters) across to about 12 feet (4 meters) across.

The ancient Yap islanders used stone money to make many different types of payments. People negotiated everyday trade with small stones, while the largest stones were used as compensation to settle disputes between villages. Yap islanders also displayed large stones outside their homes as symbols of their wealth.

*Resembling the Latin letter **M**, the mark of the ancient mint of Gaza (on the modern Gaza Strip) is located near the owl's leg on this tetradrachm.*

Forgers often made bronze copies of authentic coins and then coated the counterfeit money with a liquid mixture of mercury and ground-up silver or gold. When the counterfeit coin was heated, this mixture, or **amalgam,** would spread evenly over the coin's surface. The mercury gradually evaporated under high temperatures, leaving a smooth, even coating of gold or silver. A merchant could detect a forgery only by carefully weighing the coin or by cutting through the amalgam to reveal the bronze.

Ancient Mint Marks

Small settlements within the Greek and Roman empires employed skilled minters who crafted coins almost identical to those made in the imperial capitals. For instance, minters in ancient Gaza (a city on the Gaza Strip southwest of Israel) became skilled at reproducing the Greek tetradrachm, which originated in Athens. The Gaza coin makers used the same precious metals as the Greeks, and many of the Gaza versions are hard to distinguish from the Athenian originals.

One small detail is different on the Gaza coin, however. The tetradrachms of Gaza often bear a small letter, which is equivalent to the letter *M* in the Latin alphabet. Historians believe the letter stands for Marnas, the city's patron god. Minters added this small detail, called a **mint mark,** to signify that these particular coins were minted in Gaza, rather than in Athens.

Mint marks are still used in modern times. Most coins from the United States, for example, display a tiny mark. If the letter *S* appears, the coin was minted in San Francisco. The letter *D* identifies the coin's origin as Denver. And the letter *W* signifies that the coin came from West Point, New York. If no mint mark appears, or if a *P* is visible, the coin was made in Philadelphia, the original U.S. mint. In many ways, the coins people carry today continue traditions that began more than 2,300 years ago.

The letter **D** *beneath the date on this U.S. penny indicates that the coin was minted in Denver, Colorado.*

SEAFARERS AND CONQUERORS

Some of the world's best-known coins come from seafaring nations along the Mediterranean Sea. Throughout this region, merchants and traders bought and sold wine, oil, cloth, grain, pottery, and other goods. As these wealthy trading nations expanded into the Middle East and Asia, Mediterranean coins and money systems became more widely accepted.

The Greeks

The Greek civilization developed in the area that includes modern Greece and western Turkey. The area's rugged terrain made overland travel difficult. For this reason, many Greeks settled in the fertile valleys along the Mediterranean coast and traveled by sea.

Ancient Greece consisted of several independent city-states, each of which included a city or town and surrounding villages and farmland. Each city-state operated its own port, where inspectors made sure that merchants used proper weights and measures to determine the value of gold and silver pieces. Eventually, many city-states began to mint their own coins.

Some of the earliest Greek coins were minted in the city-states of Corinth, Aegina, and Athens from about 550 B.C. to 500 B.C. Minters in Athens struck their coins with a variety of images. In Corinth and

Aegina, coins displayed each city's official seal—either Pegasus, the winged horse of Corinth, or the turtle of Aegina.

These early coins were some of the first made of pure silver. Archaeologists believe that the Greeks developed new technologies for the large-scale mining and refining of silver. The Greeks also learned to extract silver from ores (natural combinations of minerals). Greek city-states that had rich ore deposits could soon produce vast quantities of coins.

In about 510 B.C., the city-state of Athens began to mint a silver coin that clearly reflected its origins. One side depicted the helmeted head of Athena, the city's patron goddess. The other side carried an an owl, an olive branch, and

Minters in the Greek city-state of Corinth struck their coins with the image of Pegasus, a legendary winged horse. According to Greek mythology, Pegasus carried thunder and lightning bolts for Zeus, the king of the gods.

a short form of the city's name. The owl, which was the symbol of Athena, also came to represent the wealth of Athens.

Owl coins (called owls) were in great demand throughout the Mediterranean. Merchants and traders recognized the design as a guarantee of quality backed by the rich deposits of silver in Athenian mines. Many cities surrounding the Mediterranean imitated the coins, adding their own mint marks to designate the origin.

Athens continued to mint owls for more than three centuries. During this time, minters made only slight changes in the design of the owl. At one point, a wreath of laurel leaves was added to Athena's helmet and a crescent moon was engraved near the olive sprig on the reverse side.

Sometimes the Athenians had to change the metal content of the owl. In 407 B.C., for example, when Athens was at war with the city-state of Sparta, the Spartans occupied the area containing Athens's silver deposits. Needing to meet the war's expenses, Athens melted down seven gold statues and minted an emergency issue of gold owls.

The ancient Greeks, who made some of the earliest coins, built the city-state of Athens around a high, rocky hill called the Acropolis (above). Each Greek city-state minted its own coins and controlled its own ports and trade routes.

Minted in Athens in the fifth century B.C., this Athenian silver tetradrachm shows the head of Athena (above), *the city's patron goddess. An owl, the symbol of Athena, appears on the coin's reverse side* (below).

Minters shaped the first Chinese coins to look like tools, such as this spade. Many archaeologists believe the Chinese minted the world's first coins.

CHINESE INVENTIONS

The earliest articles of exchange used in China, a country in eastern Asia, included precious stones, grain, and shells. When ancient inhabitants learned how to melt down metal and shape it into objects, they began trading metal tools—such as hoes, spades, and knives—for goods and services.

As early as 1100 B.C., metalworkers started making miniatures of these tools from bronze. Minters eventually standardized the sizes of these tiny tools, and they became China's first coins. The ancient Chinese were one of two groups that independently invented coins. Lydia (an ancient kingdom in what is now Turkey), is usually credited with minting the earliest coins, but some archaeologists believe the Chinese were the earliest coin makers.

In the third century B.C., tool-shaped coins gave way to round coins with square holes in the centers. The holes enabled the money to be carried on a string. Coins of this shape, which are called *cash* in English, soon became common in many other eastern Asian countries.

In addition to their innovations with metal coins, the Chinese also invented paper money. Chinese bankers issued the earliest known notes in the eleventh century A.D. At this time, iron coins were the only official money recognized by the government. When buyers purchased expensive items, merchants were forced to accept large quantities of the heavy coins. To ease this burden, bankers offered receipts to merchants who deposited iron coins. Each receipt showed the amount of a deposit. Eventually these notes became worth the amount written on them and circulated as paper money.

The Chinese used round coins with square holes—called cash *in English—from about 200 B.C. to the early 1900s.*

Phoenician traders display their wares to the residents of the island of Cyprus. Famous for their glassware and purple dye, Phoenician merchants called at ports throughout the Mediterranean.

The Phoenicians

The Phoenicians, a nation of sea-going traders, lived in the coastal areas of present-day Syria, Lebanon, and Israel. Among prized Phoenician goods were glass and a famous purple dye. The Phoenicians sailed the length of the Mediterranean and continued westward as far as Spain. Archaeologists believe the Phoenicians were the first people to establish trading networks in the Mediterranean region.

The Phoenicians built a number of great cities on the eastern Mediterranean shore, the most important of which were the seaports of Tyre and Sidon (both in modern Lebanon). From the late fifth cen-

tury B.C. to the end of the fourth century B.C., these harbor cities prospered as centers of commerce between the Mediterranean and the Middle East. When kingdoms such as Lydia began to mint coins, the Phoenicians were quick to follow suit. Because the Phoenicians were known far and wide as able sailors and skilled merchants, their coins were popular throughout the Mediterranean.

The most famous Phoenician coin was the double shekel from Sidon. One side of this silver coin was struck with an image of the king of Persia, who ruled the eastern Mediterranean at that time. The king is shown riding a chariot (a two-wheeled war wagon) drawn by

42

several horses. A charioteer holds the reins, and a servant follows behind. On the reverse side appears a picture of a Phoenician ship, complete with oars and a row of shields for fighting sea battles.

The silver stater was an important coin minted in Tyre. The first staters were decorated with pictures of owls and dolphins, animals that had great mystical significance in ancient times. Dolphins were especially popular among seafaring people, who admired them for their speed, strength, intelligence, and playfulness.

The double shekel from Sidon, a Phoenician port, features a warship (top) and a horse-drawn chariot (below).

Later on, minters added the likeness of Tyre's patron god Melkart to the stater. Melkart is shown as a bearded man holding a bow and arrow. Mounted on a winged horse with a fish's tail, he rides over the waves of the open sea. Some scholars believe this image of Melkart symbolized the Phoenicians' skill in crossing treacherous waters.

During the fourth century B.C., Phoenicia's trade with Greece flourished. Trade was complicated, however, because each country had its own money system based on coins of different sizes and weights. Finally, in 350 B.C., the Phoenicians changed over to the Greek monetary standard. They stopped minting silver staters and began to mint coins based on the Greek money system. This change simplified the method of exchange between Phoenicians and Greeks and fur-

Minters in Sidon struck this detailed portrait of the bearded king Abdastart.

Ancient coin makers from the Phoenician city of Tyre minted this hoard of silver shekels. The coins carry an image of Hercules, a Greek hero who was admired for his strength. An eagle with a ship between its talons appears on the reverse side. Scholars believe the ship represents Tyre's seafaring activities.

ther encouraged trade between the two countries.

Bronze Coins

During the fifth century B.C., the Phoenicians began minting the first bronze coins in the Mediterranean region. These coins were worth much less than silver coins of the same size and weight. Thus, the bronze coins could be used as small change without being reduced to very tiny proportions.

At first, the Phoenician minters made bronze coins to replace only the very smallest and least valuable silver coins. By 300 B.C., however, bronze coins had become widely accepted, and minters began to strike them in larger sizes that increased their value.

The bronze coins soon replaced all small silver coins. After this change happened, the ancient

The Romans built the largest merchant fleet of ancient times. To protect the traders' valuable cargo from pirates, Roman warships (above) accompanied trading vessels during their voyages across the Mediterranean Sea.

world possessed a full-scale, three-level monetary system based on the widely differing values of gold, silver, and bronze. This system proved so well suited to the needs of everyone—from kings to farmers—that it lasted, in one form or another, until modern times.

The Romans

In 509 B.C., the Romans established a small republic on the Italian Peninsula. During the succeeding centuries, they became known as great warriors and seafarers and used their skills to conquer more land. By A.D. 100, the Romans had taken over much of the Mediterranean region and had created a vast empire that included Greece and Phoenicia, as well as Spain, northern Africa, and Britain.

Roman traders, merchants, and soldiers carried Roman coins to distant locations. Archaeologists have discovered the empire's coins as far away as Ireland, Finland, and Russia. Excavations in eastern Africa, southern India, and Pakistan have also produced considerable finds. Roman coins have even turned up in China.

Roman minters crafted their most valuable coins from gold. But the majority of Roman coins were made of silver or bronze. As silver became scarce, its value rose. The Roman government wanted its coins to maintain their worth without changing their size, so minters began adding bronze to silver. By the late third century, larger-sized bronze coins replaced Roman silver coins.

Minted in A.D. 14, this bronze Roman coin bears the inscription, SC the mint mark of the Roman Senate.

Made by the Iroquois Indians of North America, this belt contains hundreds of wampum, or shell beads.

MONEY BEADS

Native American groups that lived along the Atlantic coast crafted tiny purple and white beads called wampum. Made from seashells, these beads originally decorated clothing and other possessions. During the 1600s, the Indians—as well as settlers from Europe—began using wampum as money.

Indian artisans carved white beads from conch, whelk, and periwinkle shells. Purple beads were shaped from hard clam shells. Because these shells were very brittle, carvers needed great skill and patience to make the tiny beads. In each bead, an artist drilled a hole for stringing the wampum or for sewing it to fabric. Native Americans most often wove beads into wampum belts, which were traditionally exchanged to finalize treaties and as signs of friendship.

A silver coin crafted in 46 B.C. (right) displays the tongs, dies, and hammer of an ancient Roman mint. Coin makers used gold to craft Rome's most valuable coins, such as this solidus (below) from the fourth-century A.D.

Ancient Headlines

During the centuries of conquest, the Romans used their coins not only as money but also as a way to spread the news of a recent victory. Minters engraved their dies with pictures and words that announced significant events. For example, one seal proclaimed "Armenia and Mesopotamia Under Roman Control!," while another stated "Dacians Put Down!" Traders brought these minted news flashes to all corners of the Roman Empire.

The most famous example of these headlines announces the defeat of the Jews, who lived in Judaea (a part of modern Israel). Because the Romans had to fight long and hard to conquer Judaea, they wanted the news of their victory to be spread quickly. For this reason, they issued a very large series of coins, each of which proclaimed "Judaea Captured!" One such coin shows a Roman soldier standing near a palm tree, a symbol of Judaea. The soldier guards a captive Jewish woman, who weeps as

The ancient Romans minted coins to advertise their conquests. This bronze coin, which declares in Latin "Judaea Captured!," announces the takeover of the Judaean capital of Jerusalem in A.D. 70.

she sits on a pile of weapons. Experts believe this scene was meant to symbolize the nation of Judaea mourning the destruction of the ancient capital of Jerusalem.

Another coin portrays the Roman emperor Vespasian partici-pating in a parade to celebrate the return of his victorious army. Vespasian is depicted riding in a chariot. These coins not only announced the defeat of the Jews but also warned other nations of the dangers of fighting against the Romans.

A victory parade (above) **celebrating the defeat of Judaea was carved into the Arch of Titus, which still stands in Rome. The image of Emperor Vespasian** *(right)* **riding in the parade appears on coins minted throughout the Roman Empire.**

HOARDS AND TREASURES

In ancient times, banks did not exist. People could not deposit their coins in one location and feel that their money was safe. Instead, people often hid their money within walls or buried it in the ground. Sometimes they simply carried their coins. Because coins were made of metals that corroded (rotted) slowly—if at all—they could be safely stored almost anywhere.

Most of these **hoards** (hidden supplies) were eventually taken from their hiding places for spending. But some money remained hidden until its discovery by archaeologists hundreds or thousands of years later.

Archaeologists identify three basic types of hoards—savings hoards, emergency hoards, and purse hoards. Savings hoards usually include high-value coins made of pure gold or pure silver. This kind of hoard often contains an even sum of money, which ancient people saved to pay for something specific, such as a religious tax or a tithe (a payment to support a church or temple).

Emergency hoards, on the other hand, usually contain a random sum of money and include coins of many different values. Because ancient people often buried or hid all their valuables during an emergency—such as a war—archaeologists also find jewelry and objects made from precious metals with emergency coins.

Archaeologists discovered this hoard of silver shekels—which range in date from A.D. 66 to A.D. 70—in an oil lamp. Ancient people, who did not have banks in which to store their money, hid coins to keep them safe from thieves and invaders.

In general, clothing in ancient times did not have pockets. Instead, ancient people carried small numbers of coins in cloth purses, which sometimes got lost or stolen. When archaeologists find a compact mass of coins, the stash is often piled in the shape of a purse. Over time, the cloth that held the ancient money broke down in the soil and disappeared. From these purse hoards, archaeologists can learn about the everyday coins that people carried.

Hiding Places

Some archaeologists have found large, valuable hoards left by owners who died without revealing where the treasure was hidden. In

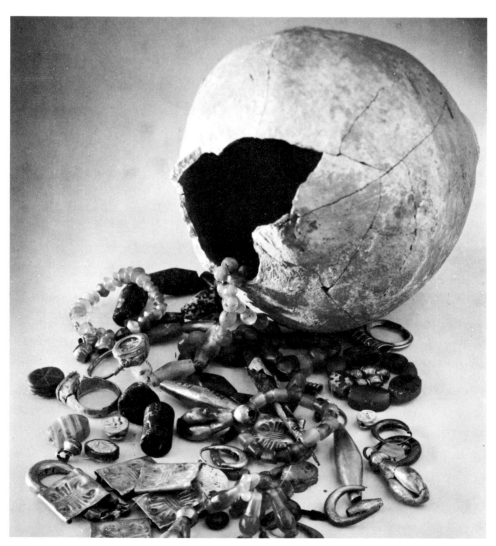

Along with coins, ancient people also hoarded jewelry and other valuables.

The stone foundations of an early settlement stand on Delos, a Greek island in the Aegean Sea. Archaeologists often find hoards stashed in the walls of ancient houses.

other cases, people may have concealed their money so well that they themselves were unable to find it later on. When war broke out, ancient people often hid their money to keep it out of the hands of enemy soldiers. Because soldiers often captured or killed people, the whereabouts of the victims' hoards were unknown until modern times.

In many early cultures, people buried their dead with money, believing that it would be needed in the afterlife. Diggers have unearthed many graves in which people were buried with coins in their mouths. Some of these early peoples may have believed that their dead needed money to pay for entrance into the next world.

Many hoards have been recovered from ancient synagogues (Jewish places of prayer), where people buried their donations under floors or hid them in the walls. In other cases, archaeologists have discovered ancient coins scattered over a wide area where pools had once existed. Apparently, people in ancient times—as they do today—threw coins into pools and fountains.

A group of archaeology students (above) **excavates (unearths) ruins in Caesarea, an ancient port city in Israel. The students uncovered a hoard of fourth-century Roman gold coins** *(left).*

A numismatist organizes his collection by packaging and labeling each coin.

COLLECTING HISTORY

Coin collecting—formally called numismatics—is one of the most popular hobbies in the world. People collect coins for a variety of reasons. Some collectors see coins as works of art. Others seek valuable coins as investments. Many numismatists simply want to learn about the famous people or events portrayed on coins.

Coin collectors can create many different types of collections. They can concentrate on coins from one country, for example, or can collect money of unusual shapes or sizes. Some numismatists gather only ancient coins or search for coins that show a certain subject, such as animals.

To help build their collections, numismatists consult magazines that specialize in coins. Books list coin prices that are based on the condition of the money. For example, coins that are rated as "fair" are worn but can still be identified by their design. Coins rated as "extremely fine," on the other hand, look almost new.

Collectors obtain coins from many sources. Beginning numismatists search the change they receive from making purchases, swap coins with their friends, or exchange money for other coins at a bank. As collectors learn more about numismatics, they begin to contact coin dealers or to attend auctions, where coins go to the highest bidder. In addition, many governments offer commemorative coins, which celebrate special events.

Tossed by the waves of the open sea, many ancient merchant ships sank to the ocean floor with their cargo and money intact.

Sunken Treasure

When ancient trading ships traveled from port to port, they carried huge quantities of wares, such as wine, grain, pottery, and animal hides. As a result, large amounts of money changed hands. This money, consisting mostly of gold and silver coins, was often placed in strongboxes for safekeeping.

Many of these ships, however, never reached their home ports. Sudden, violent storms whipped up thrashing waves that destroyed many of the light wooden trading vessels. Their cargo—including the strongboxes—sank to the bottom of the sea. Some of these hoards have been retrieved by underwater archaeologists. But hundreds more shipwrecks throughout the world remain to be explored.

Lessons of the Ancient Hoards

Many people dream of becoming rich by finding buried treasure, especially hoards containing gold and silver coins. But historians and archaeologists are thrilled when anyone turns up a new hoard to study. A large group of coins sometimes can provide clues to the past that might not make sense if the same coins had been found one by one.

For example, a hoard can reveal how long certain coins continued to be used. One hoard found near Tiberias in northern Israel contained many coins with portraits of Alexander the Great that were minted around 300 B.C. Therefore, archaeologists know that the hoard was buried sometime after that date.

But other coins in the hoard came from a much earlier time, when Tiberias was controlled by the Persian Empire. The Persian coins in the hoard date from as early as 400 B.C. This hoard shows that coins minted 50 or even 100 years earlier were still in use after 300 B.C.

Besides providing information about how and when certain coins were used, hoards can also give us information about other aspects of ancient life. The engravings of ancient galley ships and of signs of the zodiac, for instance, tell us much about the seafaring life and the religious beliefs of the past.

Ancient coins and other types of money exist all over the world. Each kind helps us to trace the history of people, events, and artistic styles. In modern times, money still carries important information. As a result, future generations will be able to examine our coins to learn about the people and events that have shaped our lives.

An underwater archaeologist probes the remains of a shipwreck. Coins, which can usually be traced to a certain time and place, help excavators identify when a ship sank.

PRONUNCIATION GUIDE

Accho (ah-KOH)

Aegina (ih-JY-nuh)

Ashqelon (ASH-kuh-lahn)

Hadrian (HAY-dree-uhn)

Judaea (ju-DAY-uh)

Lydia (LIHD-ee-uh)

Macedonia (mas-uh-DOH-nyuh)

Mesopotamia (mehs-uh-puh-TAY-mee-uh)

Phoenicia (fih-NEESH-uh)

Sidon (SIDE-uhn)

shekel (SHEHK-uhl)

tetradrachm (TEH-truh-dram)

Tiberias (ty-BEER-ee-uhs)

Tyre (TY-uhr)

Vespasian (veh-SPAY-zhuhn)

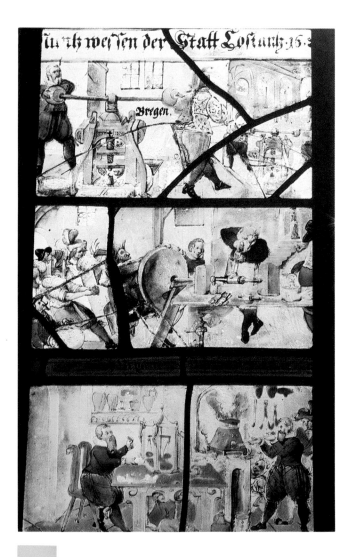

Scenes on a stained-glass window depict activity at a German mint in the 1600s.

GLOSSARY

amalgam: a mixture of mercury with one or more other metals.

anvil: a heavy, sturdy object—such as a tree stump or an iron block—on which heated metal objects can be pounded or hammered into a desired shape.

archaeologist: a scientist who studies the material remains of past human life.

barter: a system of trade in which goods and services are paid for with other goods and services instead of with money.

cast: a mold into which a liquid substance—such as heated metal—is poured. When cooled or dried, the liquid hardens into the shape of the mold.

die: a tool that presses or strikes an object to give it a certain shape or form. A die can punch holes in metal or stamp designs on coins.

electrum: a natural metal that contains both gold and silver.

flan: a round, flat metal disk onto which a design is stamped to make a coin or medal.

hoard: a supply of money or other valuable objects that has been stored or hidden.

ingot: a molded bar or other solid mass of metal, such as gold, silver, or bronze.

Newly made coins at a U.S. mint are screened through a vibrating machine. This process removes coins that are not the proper size.

mint: to make coins out of metal. A mint is also a place where money is made.

mint mark: a symbol stamped on a coin to identify where the coin was made.

seal: a symbol, word, or other mark stamped on a coin, document, or other object to show that the item is genuine and valuable.

striking: the act of stamping a design on a coin or other object.

INDEX

Workers trim the edges of U.S. paper money produced in 1907. All U.S. paper currency is printed at the Bureau of Engraving and Printing in Washington, D.C.

Before making a purchase, a woman carefully examines fabrics at a merchant's shop in ancient Athens.

Photo Acknowledgments

Z. Radovan, Jerusalem, pp. 2, 11, 17 (top), 45, 50, 53; Independent Picture Service, pp. 7, 12, 15, 16, 18 (top and bottom), 20, 22, 25, 26 (top and bottom), 27, 30, 31 (top and bottom), 34, 35, 38, 42, 43, 44, 46, 51 (top and bottom), 54, 59; British Museum, pp. 8, 33, 48; Museum of the American Numismatic Association, pp. 10, 40; William E. Daehn, pp. 13, 17 (bottom), 21 (top), 32, 39 (top and bottom); James Marrinan, pp. 19, 21 (bottom), 37, 47; The Mansell Collection, pp. 29, 58; National Museum of History, Taiwan, p. 41; American Numismatic Society, pp.9, 49 (top and bottom); Meredith Pillon/Greek National Tourist Organization, p. 55; Dr. Olin Storvick, Joint Expedition to Caesarea Maritima, pp. 23, 56 (top and bottom); Coin World, p. 57; Rosgarten Museum, Konstanz, p. 60; The United States Mint at Denver, p. 61; National Archives, p. 62; The Bettmann Archive, p. 63.

Cover photographs: Museum of the American Numismatic Association (front) and Dr. Olin Storvick, Joint Expedition to Caesarea Maritima (back).